Los Angeles Area Missions

Exploring CALIFORNIA MISSIONS

❖

BY
DIANNE M. MACMILLAN

❖

CONSULTANT:
JAMES J. RAWLS, PH.D.
PROFESSOR EMERITUS
DEPARTMENT OF HISTORY
DIABLO VALLEY COLLEGE

LERNER PUBLICATIONS COMPANY/MINNEAPOLIS

The images in this book are used with permission of: © North Wind Picture Archives, pp. 6, 14, 22, 40, 47; © Eda Rogers, pp. 8, 35, 36, 38, 57; San Diego Museum of Man, p. 10; © Marilyn "Angel" Wynn/Nativestock.com, p. 11; Courtesy of the Bancroft Library, University of California, Berkeley, pp. 12, 34, 48, 52; Collection of the Santa Barbara Historical Society, p. 15; © Lake County Museum/CORBIS, p. 16; © age fotostock/SuperStock, p. 18; © Richard Cummins/CORBIS, p. 21; Zephyrin Engelhardt, The Missions and Missionaries of California, 1908-1915, pp. 23, 26, 43; © Tom Brakefield/SuperStock, p. 29; Ventura County Museum of History and Art, p. 31; © Charles Fredeen, p. 32; California Historical Society, Title Insurance and Trust Photo Collection, Department of Special Collections, University of Southern California Library, pp. 37, 53; The Huntington Library, San Marino, CA, pp. 42, 46; Library of Congress, p. 45 (LC-USZ62-108463); Special Collections, Tutt Library, Colorado College, Colorado Springs, CO, p. 49; Seaver Center for Western History, Los Angeles County Museum of Natural History, pp. 50, 54, 55; © Diane C. Lyell, p. 56. Illustrations on pp. 4, 13, 25, 58, 59 by © Laura Westlund/Independent Picture Service.

Front cover: © age fotostock/SuperStock.
Back cover: © Laura Westlund/Independent Picture Service.

Lerner Publications Company
A division of Lerner Publishing Group, Inc.
241 First Avenue North
Minneapolis, MN 55401 U.S.A.

Website address: www.lernerbooks.com

Library of Congress Cataloging-in-Publication Data

MacMillan, Dianne M., 1943–
    Los Angeles area missions / by Dianne MacMillan.
        p.   cm. — (Exploring California missions)
    Includes index.
    ISBN-13: 978-0-8225-0898-4 (lib. bdg. : alk. paper)
    1. Missions, Spanish—California—Los Angeles Region—History—Juvenile literature. 2. Los Angeles Region (Calif.)—History, Local—Juvenile literature. 3. Mission San Gabriel Arcangel (San Gabriel, Calif.)—History—Juvenile literature. 4. San Buenaventura Mission—History—Juvenile literature. 5. San Fernando, Rey de España (Mission : San Fernando, Calif.)—History—Juvenile literature. 6. Spanish mission buildings—California—Los Angeles Region—Juvenile literature. 7. Indians of North America—Missions—California—Los Angeles Region—History—Juvenile literature. 8. California—History—To 1846—Juvenile literature. I. Title.
F869.L88A238 2008
979.4'94—dc22   2006039020

Manufactured in the United States of America
1 2 3 4 5 6 – DP – 13 12 11 10 09 08

CONTENTS

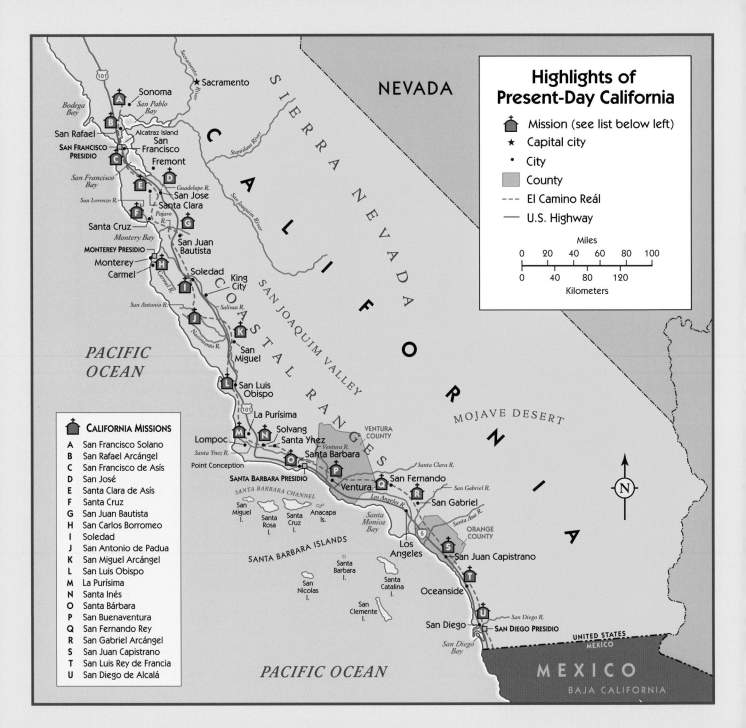

Highlights of Present-Day California

- 🏠 Mission (see list below left)
- ★ Capital city
- • City
- County
- --- El Camino Reál
- — U.S. Highway

Miles
0 20 40 60 80 100

0 40 80 120
Kilometers

California Missions

- **A** San Francisco Solano
- **B** San Rafael Arcángel
- **C** San Francisco de Asís
- **D** San José
- **E** Santa Clara de Asís
- **F** Santa Cruz
- **G** San Juan Bautista
- **H** San Carlos Borromeo
- **I** Soledad
- **J** San Antonio de Padua
- **K** San Miguel Arcángel
- **L** San Luis Obispo
- **M** La Purísima
- **N** Santa Inés
- **O** Santa Bárbara
- **P** San Buenaventura
- **Q** San Fernando Rey
- **R** San Gabriel Arcángel
- **S** San Juan Capistrano
- **T** San Luis Rey de Francia
- **U** San Diego de Alcalá

NEVADA

PACIFIC OCEAN

CALIFORNIA

SIERRA NEVADA

COASTAL RANGES

SAN JOAQUIM VALLEY

MOJAVE DESERT

Sacramento

Bodega Bay
Sonoma
San Pablo Bay
San Rafael
Alcatraz Island
San Francisco
SAN FRANCISCO PRESIDIO
Fremont
San Francisco Bay
San Jose
Santa Clara
San Lorenzo R.
Santa Cruz
Monterey Bay
San Juan Bautista
MONTEREY PRESIDIO
Monterey
Carmel
Soledad
King City
San Antonio R.
San Miguel
San Luis Obispo
La Purísima
Lompoc
Solvang
Santa Ynez
Santa Barbara
SANTA BARBARA PRESIDIO
Point Conception
Ventura
VENTURA COUNTY
San Fernando
Los Angeles
San Gabriel
ORANGE COUNTY
San Juan Capistrano
Oceanside
San Diego
SAN DIEGO PRESIDIO

Sacramento River
Stanislaus River
Guadelupe R.
Pajaro R.
Carmel R.
Salinas R.
Nacimiento R.
San Joaquin River
Santa Ynez R.
Ventura R.
Santa Clara R.
San Gabriel R.
Los Angeles R.
Santa Ana R.
San Diego R.

SANTA BARBARA CHANNEL
San Miguel I.
Santa Rosa I.
Santa Cruz I.
Anacapa Is.
Santa Monica Bay
SANTA BARBARA ISLANDS
Santa Barbara I.
San Nicolas I.
Santa Catalina I.
San Clemente I.

San Diego Bay

PACIFIC OCEAN

UNITED STATES
MEXICO
MEXICO
BAJA CALIFORNIA

N

INTRODUCTION

Spain and the Roman Catholic Church built twenty California **missions** between 1769 and 1817. A final mission was built in 1823. The missions stand along a narrow strip of California's Pacific coast. Today, the missions sit near Highway 101. They are between the cities of San Diego and Sonoma.

The Spaniards built **presidios** (forts) and missions throughout their empire. This system helped the Spanish claim and protect new lands. In California, the main goal of the mission system was to control Native Americans and their lands. The Spaniards wanted Native Americans to accept their leadership and way of life.

Spanish **missionaries** and soldiers ran the presidio and mission system. Father Junípero Serra was the missions' first leader. He was called father-president. Father Serra and the other priests taught Native Americans the Catholic faith. The priests showed them how to behave like Spaniards. The soldiers made sure Native Americans obeyed the priests.

The area was home to many Native American groups. They had their own beliefs and practices. The Spanish ways were much different from their own. Some Native Americans willingly joined the missions. But others did not. They did not want to give up their own ways of life.

The Spaniards tried different methods to make Native Americans join their missions. Sometimes they gave the Native Americans gifts. Other times, the Spanish used force. To stay alive, the Native Americans had no choice but to join the missions.

The Spanish called Native Americans who joined their missions **neophytes.** The Spaniards taught neophytes the Catholic religion. The neophytes built buildings and farmed the land. They also produced goods, such as cloth and soap. They built a trade route connecting the missions. It was called El Camino Reál (the Royal Road). The goods and trade were expected to earn money and power for Spain.

Spanish missionary Father Garzes instructs Native Americans.

But the system did not last. More than half of the Native Americans died from diseases the Spaniards brought. Mexico took control of the area in 1821 and closed the missions. Neophytes were free to leave or stay at the missions. In 1848, the United States gained control of California. Some of the remaining neophytes returned to their people. But many others had no people to return to. They moved to **pueblos** (towns) or inland areas. The missions sat empty. They fell apart over time.

This book is about three missions in the Los Angeles area of California. Spanish missionaries built San Gabriel Arcángel, San Buenaventura, and San Fernando Rey de España.

CALIFORNIA MISSION	FOUNDING DATE
San Diego de Alcalá	July 16, 1769
San Carlos Borromeo de Carmelo	June 3, 1770
San Antonio de Padua	July 14, 1771
San Gabriel Arcángel	September 8, 1771
San Luis Obispo de Tolosa	September 1, 1772
San Francisco de Asís	June 29, 1776
San Juan Capistrano	November 1, 1776
Santa Clara de Asís	January 12, 1777
San Buenaventura	March 31, 1782
Santa Bárbara Virgen y Mártir	December 4, 1786
La Purísima Concepción de Maria Santísima	December 8, 1787
Santa Cruz	August 28, 1791
Nuestra Señora de la Soledad	October 9, 1791
San José	June 11, 1797
San Juan Bautista	June 24, 1797
San Miguel Arcángel	July 25, 1797
San Fernando Rey de España	September 8, 1797
San Luis Rey de Francia	June 13, 1798
Santa Inés Virgen y Mártir	September 17, 1804
San Rafael Arcángel	December 14, 1817
San Francisco Solano	July 4, 1823

Huge oak trees spread their leaves over the dry, grassy area of what has become modern-day Los Angeles.

·1·

EARLY LIFE ALONG THE COAST

Los Angeles, California, is known for its gleaming skyscrapers and crowded freeways. But thousands of years ago, this area was far different. Antelope grazed in grassy meadows. Rabbits lived beneath giant oak trees. Whales, dolphins, sharks, and shellfish swam in the Pacific Ocean.

The area was also home to many Native Americans (also called American Indians). There were two main groups in the Los Angeles area. They were the Chumash and the Tongva.

These people felt a close connection to Earth and other living things. They believed that each plant, animal, mountain, lake, and river had a spirit. They treated these spirits with respect. And they took only what they needed to live.

The Chumash people lived in villages along the Pacific coast. These villages stretched north from modern-day Ventura County to central California. The Chumash also lived on islands near the coast.

The Tongva people lived south of the Chumash. Their villages covered much of modern-day Los Angeles. They also lived in San Fernando and Orange County. The Tongva had villages on Santa Catalina and other islands too.

Deer-hoof rattles were used in special rituals and celebrations.

NATIVE AMERICAN LIFE

Nature provided everything the Chumash and Tongva needed. They drank from the rivers and streams. Women gathered acorns, berries, and seaweed for food. Men brought home game and fish.

The Chumash and Tongva made clothing and blankets from feathers and animal skins. They built homes shaped like domes from young trees and stiff reeds.

The Tongva and Chumash made homes by covering a dome of wicker branches with grass.

Before hunting or sacred ceremonies, Chumash and Tongva men purified themselves in a sweat lodge.

The day's work depended on the season and the people's needs. If people were hungry, they looked for food. If they were tired, they rested.

Villagers started the day by bathing in a stream. Chumash and Tongva men also liked sweat baths. They went into a small building the Spanish called a *temescal*, or sweat lodge. There, the men gathered around a hot fire. They got hot and sweaty. Then they jumped into the ocean or a cool stream.

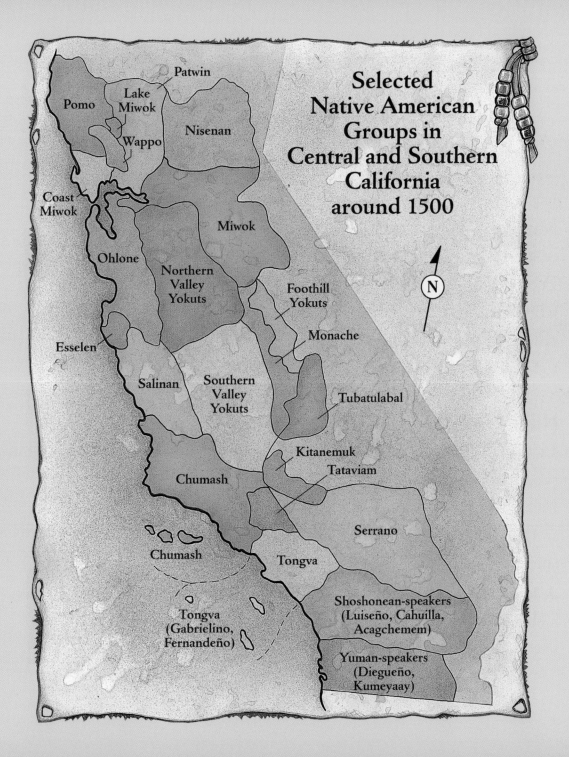

Selected
Native American
Groups in
Central and Southern
California
around 1500

N

Patwin
Lake Miwok
Pomo
Wappo
Nisenan
Coast Miwok
Ohlone
Miwok
Northern Valley Yokuts
Foothill Yokuts
Monache
Esselen
Salinan
Southern Valley Yokuts
Tubatulabal
Kitanemuk
Tataviam
Chumash
Serrano
Chumash
Tongva
Shoshonean-speakers
(Luiseño, Cahuilla, Acagchemem)
Tongva
(Gabrielino, Fernandeño)
Yuman-speakers
(Diegueño, Kumeyaay)

13

Art and music were important parts of village life. Craftspeople carved wooden boats and wove baskets. They also shaped beautiful containers from wood or stone. People used shells as money. And they made jewelry from shells. Musicians played flutes and other instruments and shook rattles. People sang songs as a way to teach, worship, and celebrate. Village elders told stories to teach children the history of their people.

NEWCOMERS

In 1542, Juan Rodríguez Cabrillo sailed north from **Baja California**. Baja California was part of a Spanish settlement called **New Spain** (modern-day Mexico). Cabrillo's job was to explore the coast of Alta California (modern-day California). Native Americans greeted Cabrillo

Juan Rodríguez Cabrillo was a Portugese explorer who worked for the Spanish government.

The Chumash made canoes, called *tomols*, for fishing and travel. When the Spaniards arrived, the Chumash paddled out to meet them.

and his crew. They gave the Spaniards food and water. The Spaniards gave the Native Americans beads and other gifts in return. Cabrillo claimed Alta California for Spain. He did this even though people were already living there.

In 1769, the king of Spain decided it was time to do something with this land. He sent Captain Gaspar de Portolá and a group of soldiers to Alta California. They were to set up presidios.

These forts were used to protect the land from attack. A Catholic priest named Father Junípero Serra went with them. He wanted to set up missions. Father Serra would use the missions to teach the Catholic faith.

THE MISSION SYSTEM

In 1769, Father Serra blessed a site for the first mission in Alta California. He named it San Diego de Alcalá. The priest wanted to spread his faith. He left two other priests in charge. Then he continued up the coast to set up more missions. These missions were a long way from the first Spanish settlements in San Diego.

The missions were set up to convince Native Americans to become Catholics. The priests also wanted Native Americans to become subjects of the Spanish empire and follow Spanish rule. Then Spain would have many people at its

Father Junípero Serra was fifty-six years old when he founded San Diego de Alcalá.

missions in Alta California. That would show other countries that the land belonged to Spain.

The missions needed these new Catholics to succeed. The neophytes would build the mission buildings. They would clear land and grow crops. They would also make most of the goods the settlements needed. The Spanish government would help. It would provide soldiers and a little money. It also provided a few supplies that the neophytes could not make themselves.

Spanish officials thought the neophytes could run the mission by themselves in ten years. The Catholic Church would continue to hold services in the mission churches. But the priests would turn the land over to the neophytes. The neophytes would farm the land. They would pay taxes to Spain. Then the missionaries would go off to start new missions. The priests believed they were teaching Native Americans a better way to live. They did not think that the native people had a right to live the way they wanted.

The bells of Mission
San Gabriel Arcángel

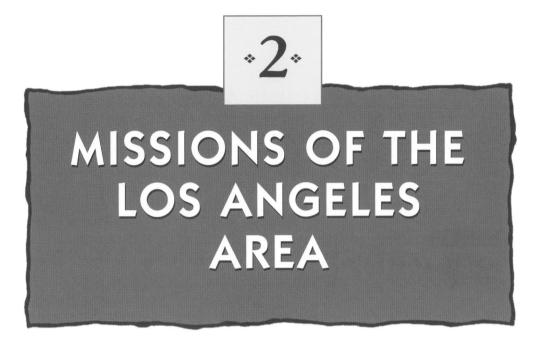

MISSIONS OF THE LOS ANGELES AREA

Father Serra knew that a successful mission needed good soil. It also needed plenty of water. Most of all, it needed lots of workers. The Spaniards looked for sites near large Native American villages. Over the next two years, Father Serra founded two missions. They were near the presidio at Monterey Bay. But these missions were a long way from San Diego. The Spaniards needed to reach out to the many Native Americans living in between.

❖❖❖

MISSION SAN GABRIEL ARCÁNGEL

On September 8, 1771, a group of Spaniards arrived in the area we know as Los Angeles. Soon after, a group of Tongva Indians with bows and arrows surrounded their camp. One of the frightened priests held out a painting of Mary, the mother of Jesus. The Tongva set down their weapons. They placed their necklaces on the ground in front of the painting.

Some historians believe that the Tongva were honoring Chukit, a female spirit. But the priests thought that the Native Americans were accepting the Catholic faith. Father Ángel Somera and Father Pedro Benito Cambón pounded a wooden cross into the ground. They blessed the site of Mission San Gabriel Arcángel. It was the fourth mission in Alta California.

Native Americans in the area came to see what the Spaniards were doing. The Spaniards were friendly. They offered them gifts of beads and clothing. In return, the American Indians helped them to build some basic shelters and a chapel.

A statue of Father Serra watches over the entrance to the church at San Gabriel.

PROBLEMS AT THE START

Not long after its founding, the mission ran into trouble. A Spanish soldier attacked the wife of a Tongva chief. The people of the Tongva village tried to kill the soldier. But they were no match for the Spaniards. Soldiers cut off the chief's head. They put it on a pole. After that, the Tongva stayed away. But soldiers still attacked villagers. The priests complained to the government. But officials did little to keep the soldiers in line.

It didn't help that San Gabriel's priests became ill. Soon two new priests arrived to take over. Father Antonio Cruzado and Father Antonio Paterna wanted to patch up the mission's relationship with the Tongva. But few people were willing to join the mission.

Priests weren't the only ones in California who got sick. Diseases that came to Alta California with the Europeans spread to local villages. These diseases were new to Native Americans. Their bodies could not fight off the diseases. Many Native Americans died, especially children.

The priests at San Gabriel traveled to local villages and performed baptisms. They believed that people who were

A few Native Americans chose to become Catholics and wear European clothing.

A priest baptizes a Native American baby. This ceremony welcomed the baby into the Catholic Church.

baptized would go to heaven when they died. Baptized children were forced to live at the mission. Their parents had to join the mission too if they wanted to be with their children. The mission finally began to grow.

MISSION LIFE

The neophytes at San Gabriel had lots of work to do. They built a church and living quarters. They also built a granary for storing grain. These buildings were arranged in a rectangle. An open space was in the center. This arrangement was called a **quadrangle**.

Workers cleared trees and rocks. They learned to plant wheat, corn, and vegetables. But floods destroyed the mission's first crops. There was not enough food for everyone. The priests had to rely on the neophytes' old ways to find food.

In 1775, the priests decided to move the mission to a new site five miles away. This site had rich soil. And it was less likely to flood. The mission soon had lush fields of wheat and corn. Later, the neophytes grew grapes, olives, and other fruits.

More neophytes joined the mission. Workers added more living quarters. They built more storehouses and workshops. Many of these newer buildings were made of **adobe**. Adobe is a kind of clay soil. Workers mixed the adobe with straw and water. They poured the mixture into molds. Then they let them bake in the sun. The clay became dry, hard adobe bricks.

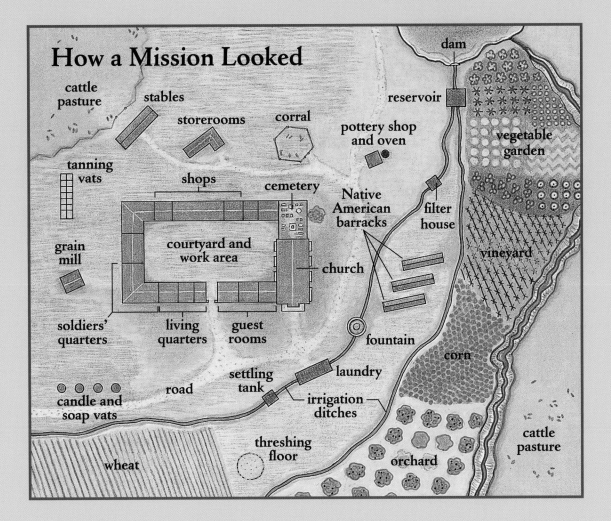

How a Mission Looked

cattle pasture

stables

storerooms

corral

pottery shop and oven

reservoir

dam

vegetable garden

tanning vats

shops

cemetery

Native American barracks

filter house

grain mill

courtyard and work area

church

vineyard

soldiers' quarters

living quarters

guest rooms

fountain

corn

candle and soap vats

road

settling tank

laundry

irrigation ditches

cattle pasture

wheat

threshing floor

orchard

At the missions, neophyte men farmed the land.

Neophyte men did most of the building. They also tended herds of sheep, goats, and cattle. They tanned cattle hides to produce leather. The women fed the people at the growing mission. They learned to make Spanish foods. The women made flat circles of bread called tortillas. They also made a beef-and-corn stew called posole. Even neophyte children had jobs to do. Boys helped the men with the crops and livestock. Girls helped the women spin yarn, weave cloth, and sew clothing and blankets. They used tallow to make soap and candles. Tallow is fat from cattle.

Girls and unmarried women did most of their work in a building called a *monjerio*. They ate and slept in this hot, crowded space too. The doors were locked at night. That kept the women in and the men out. Without fresh air or regular baths, many women and girls at San Gabriel got sick and died.

Some neophytes probably joined the mission because they liked the church music. They also liked the gifts the Spaniards gave them. The American Indians had no idea how much their lives would be changed. Bells rang to tell everyone when to wake up. Bells also told them when to eat, pray, work, and sleep. The priests made neophytes attend church services. But they didn't understand the Latin and Spanish words. Mission rules kept American Indians from practicing their own religion. They could not play their own music either. They could not even leave the mission to visit family and friends.

When neophytes didn't work hard or when they broke the rules (and sometimes even when they didn't), they were punished harshly. If they ran away, soldiers went after them. The soldiers brought them back and beat them. In 1785, a neophyte named Nicolas José made a plan to get rid of the Spaniards. Soldiers found out about the plan and punished him.

SUCCESS AT SAN GABRIEL

In 1791, the mission was running smoothly. Father Cruzado made plans for a new church. The Spanish-style stone and brick building wasn't completed until 1804. Father Cruzado had died one year earlier. A large earthquake in 1812 damaged the building. But even that didn't slow the mission's progress.

The new priest, Father José María Zalvidea, was a strict man. He gave some neophytes the job of beating those who didn't work hard enough. Soon San Gabriel earned the nickname the Pride of the Missions. It ran a respected winery. It raised huge herds of livestock. And it produced more grain than any farm in Alta California. In workshops, neophytes produced candles, ironwork, and other supplies. Many of the mission's extra goods were sold to the public. They were sold in the nearby pueblo of Nuestra Señora la Reina de los Angeles del Río de Porciúncula, also known as Los Angeles.

Yet nothing could stop the diseases that swept through the mission. In 1825, three out of every four neophytes died of smallpox or cholera. In all, six thousand people were buried at Mission San Gabriel.

Mission San Buenaventura has a bell tower with a domed roof.

❖❖❖

MISSION SAN BUENAVENTURA

Father Serra had always been eager to start a mission in Chumash territory. It lay halfway between San Diego and Monterey. But problems with money and politics forced him to wait. On March 31, 1782, he finally got his wish. Mission San Buenaventura was the ninth mission in Alta California. Seventy soldiers and their families were on hand for the seaside ceremony.

Father Serra chose Father Cambón to head the new mission. Father Cambón had founded Mission San Gabriel eleven years earlier. He was also an expert on irrigation, or the watering of crops. That knowledge would come in handy. San Buenaventura had water problems. The mission could draw drinking water from several creeks. But there were no larger water sources nearby to support a farm.

BUILDING THE MISSION

Once again, the priests gave the local people gifts in exchange for help with the first mission buildings. But the Chumash were not interested in joining the mission. In the first nine months, San Buenaventura had just two baptisms. After two years, only twenty-two neophytes lived at the mission. The priests had no choice. They had to hire people to build the mission. In payment, the workers received useful goods, such as knives, axes, and needles.

By 1790, the mission's quadrangle included granaries, homes, and priests' quarters. Soon after, workers began to build an adobe church. The other big project at the mission was the water system. Father Cambón had to find a way to direct water to the mission. The water would come from the Ventura River, five miles away.

Parts of San Buenaventura's water system, including the aqueduct wall (*right*), still remain.

In the early years of the mission, workers dug simple ditches from the river to the fields. They made dams from logs and brush. The dams forced river water to flow into the ditches. In the early 1790s, experts from New Spain taught the neophytes how to make the dams stronger. Then they designed an **aqueduct**. This was a system of rock-lined ditches and clay pipes. Water in the aqueduct always flowed slowly downhill, even when it crossed hills and valleys.

Sections of the aqueduct pipes can still be seen in the areas around San Buenaventura.

When the water reached the mission, some of the water flowed through a screen. The screen trapped dirt, rocks, and other unwanted materials. The neophytes used this clean water for drinking and cooking. The rest of the water was stored in pools called reservoirs. From there, workers directed water to farm fields, orchards, or one of several washbasins. People used these basins for bathing or washing clothes.

With a ready supply of water, the neophytes at San Buenaventura raised crops. They raised grapes, olives, bananas, sugarcane, dates, and pomegranates. In 1793, a visitor reported that the mission's gardens were the finest he had ever seen.

MISSION LIFE

In 1806, San Buenaventura welcomed a new priest, Father José Señán. He served as head of the mission for seventeen years. During some of this time, he also served as president of all the California missions.

Father Señán felt that the mission would be more successful if the neophytes had more freedom. He let them build sweat lodges. He encouraged them to grow their favorite foods. He even let them decorate a fountain with a traditional statue of a bear instead of a Catholic saint. Yet San Buenaventura still had many strict rules. Any neophyte who ran away was beaten or put in jail.

In 1812, a large earthquake damaged the mission's aqueduct and buildings. Father Señán moved the mission a few miles away while the neophytes made repairs. The mission continued to grow. By 1816, more than thirteen hundred neophytes belonged to the mission.

In 1818, the people of San Buenaventura had to leave again. The mission got news that a pirate named Hippolyte de Bouchard was coming. The neophytes hid their valuables. They fled into the hills with their livestock. They returned a month later. The mission was unharmed.

Father Senán died in 1823. His fellow priests and the neophytes mourned his death. The kindly priest had left his mark on the lovely place known as the Mission by the Bay.

This sketch of San Buenaventura in 1829 shows the large cross on the hill above the mission.

The priests' quarters at Mission San Fernando have a long, shaded porch.

❖❖❖

MISSION SAN FERNANDO REY DE ESPAÑA

On September 8, 1797, Father Fermín Francisco de Lasuén blessed the site for Mission San Fernando Rey de España. Father Lasuén had been the president of the missions since 1784, when Father Serra died. The new mission was located halfway between the San Gabriel and San Buenaventura missions.

Fathers Francisco Dumetz and Juan Cortés had no trouble attracting Tongva to the mission. Many of the people were hungry. Mission San Gabriel had overtaken most of their hunting and gathering grounds. Joining a mission often seemed the only way to survive.

BUILDING THE MISSION

San Fernando had a founding ceremony. At that time, several Tongva families had their children baptized. Within two months, forty Tongva were living at the mission. In just one year, the neophytes built a church, a storeroom, a weaving room, and a granary. Soon after, they added more workshops. They also built barracks for the soldiers.

Neophytes decorated doors and walls with wavy lines as a common theme.

Juan Antonio's paintings of the stations of the cross may be the first mural painted in the Los Angeles area.

In 1800, workers built a bigger church. Soon the population reached one thousand. Workers completed an even larger church in 1806. There, a talented neophyte artist named Juan Antonio painted the fourteen stations of the cross. These paintings showed the events leading up to the death of Jesus. The face of Jesus in the paintings has Native American features. Some people believe this shows that Juan Antonio had accepted the Catholic faith as his own. Others believe that he was comparing the suffering of Jesus to the suffering of the neophytes.

In 1810, neophytes started to build a *convento*. In this building, the priests would live and work. The convento faced a road called El Camino Reál. Tired travelers began to stop and spend the night. Workers kept adding more rooms. Twelve years later, the convento was finally finished. It measured 243 feet long and 50 feet wide. Known as the long building, it had more than twenty rooms.

Visitors entered the convento through giant double doors. A priest greeted the visitors in the *sala*, or main room. He offered them a basin and a pitcher of water for washing up. Then guests could enjoy a glass of wine. There was no charge to stay at the mission, so the sala was always busy.

Fancy iron grills decorate the windows at Mission San Fernando.

MISSION LIFE

Mission San Fernando grew into a successful farm and ranch. At its peak, the mission owned as many as 13,000 cattle, 8,000 sheep, and 2,300 horses. It became famous for its hides and tallow. Neophytes made thin strips of hide. The strips were used in place of nails to hold boards together. Tanners turned hides into leather for shoes and saddles. The mission also made iron tools, cloth, brick, tile, olive oil, wine, and soap.

Keeping the mission running smoothly meant long workdays for the neophytes. Some people refused to work or worked very slowly. This was a way to fight the mission system. Often soldiers punished the workers by whipping them in front of the other neophytes. That way, everyone could see what would happen if they broke the rules.

Some neophytes ran away. Others became sick and died. By 1811, the number of neophytes at San Fernando began to drop. When the 1812 earthquake damaged mission buildings, repair work was slow. Mission San Fernando never recovered.

In the late 1820s, Mission San Gabriel was able to support itself. It had productive lands and many workers.

❖3❖

STATE CONTROL OF THE MISSIONS

The neophytes were not the only people who were unhappy with their Spanish leaders. In 1810, the people of New Spain went to war against Spain. In 1821, they won their freedom. Baja California and Alta California became a new territory. It became part of the Republic of Mexico. The missions still belonged to the Catholic Church. But they stood on Mexican soil.

The Mexican government moved quickly to protect its claim to Alta California. Mexican leaders urged people to move there and start farms and ranches.

The Mexican settlers wanted land that was good for farming and ranching.

These settlers were called **Californios**. They complained bitterly to the government that the missions already owned the best farmland.

In the 1830s, the Mexican government began to pass laws to take the missions away from the Catholic Church. This process was called **secularization**. The government replaced the Spanish missionaries with Mexican priests. The new priests held services. But they no longer had the power to force Native Americans to remain at the mission. The neophytes were free to leave.

The Mexican government hired people called civil administrators. They divided the missions' property. The civil administrators were supposed to give some of the land to neophytes and to sell the rest. But most of the administrators did not divide the land fairly. They took the best land for themselves and for their friends and family.

A civil administrator encourages former neophytes to find work away from the mission.

Few neophytes received anything. Those Native Americans who did receive land usually did not own it for long. Californios tried to trick them into selling it at low prices.

Even without land of their own, some neophytes were glad to be free. But many of them had no money. And they had nowhere to go. They had grown up at the missions. They had forgotten many of the skills they needed to live off the land. Their families' villages had been wiped out by disease. Some people stayed at the missions for as long as they could. Others moved away to join other Native American communities. Some took low-paying jobs on ranches or in pueblos.

SECULARIZATION AT THE LOS ANGELES MISSIONS

The three Los Angeles area missions were among the first to be secularized. In 1834, Mission San Gabriel became government property. A few neophytes were too old or sick to leave. They moved into the mission church and took care

Many Chumash left the missions and built farms and ranches like those of the Californios.

of the building. The rest of San Gabriel was not so lucky. Its sixteen thousand animals were sold or stolen. Buildings began to crumble.

San Buenaventura was closed in 1834. The six hundred neophytes at the mission were free to leave. Only the church stayed open for services. San Buenaventura was officially secularized two years later.

In March of that year, two men were arguing over who should be governor of Alta California. One of them was Carlos Carrillo, the administrator at San Buenaventura. The other was the former governor, Juan Bautista Alvarado. The two sides clashed at the mission. After two days of fighting, Carrillo and his men fled. A new administrator came to divide the property and sell it to settlers.

Governor Pío Pico sold or gave away mission lands to his friends and relatives.

Mission San Fernando was secularized in 1834. Settlers stole tiles from the church roof. They used them on their houses. Soon the building's adobe walls began to fall apart. In 1842, an administrator discovered gold near the mission. People flocked to the site. They tore up the church's floor in their search for more gold.

In 1843, Mexican government officials decided to return twelve of the missions, including San Gabriel and San Buenaventura, to the Catholic Church. But then the officials changed their minds. By 1846, Governor Pío Pico had sold San Gabriel and San Buenaventura to settlers from the United States. He kept some of the money from the sale for himself. He sold San Fernando the following year. But by this time, the ownership of Alta California was in question.

THE UNITED STATES TAKES OVER

Mexico had long argued with the United States over its **borders**. In 1846, the U.S. Congress declared war on Mexico. By 1848, the war was over. Mexico gave up control of about half its lands. On September 9, 1850, the United States made California its thirty-first state.

Prospectors came to California in search of the gold nuggets found in streams and mines.

At about the same time, thousands of people began to pour into California from the eastern United States. Some wanted to start farms. Others hoped to get rich by finding gold. They all wanted to buy land.

The U.S. government made Californios and other settlers show proof that they owned their land. Many Californios were unable to prove they owned their lands. They lost their property. Under U.S. law, Native Americans had no property rights at all. Settlers could simply take their land. Even more Native Americans became homeless.

The government decided to set aside special areas just for Native Americans. These areas, called **reservations**, were

Soldiers and civil administrators forced Native Americans to give up their land.

In 1883, these Native American women had taken over a dwelling at Mission San Gabriel.

usually no good for farming. Hunger, disease, and battles with settlers left more Native Americans dead. By the late 1860s, fewer than thirty thousand were left in California. Only a few hundred of these were Tongva and Chumash.

During the 1860s, the United States returned the mission buildings to the Catholic Church. Most of the property was badly damaged. The Catholic Church had no money for repairs.

Artist Edwin Deakin's painting of San Fernando reminded people of the beauty of the missions.

·4·

THE MISSIONS IN MODERN TIMES

For many years, people forgot about the missions. Then, in 1884, a writer named Helen Hunt Jackson wrote a book called *Ramona*. It was a story about Native Americans during mission times. Jackson wanted to show how poorly the Spaniards had treated the Native Americans. Most readers ignored that part of the story. They saw mission life as an exciting adventure. They wanted to visit the historic sites. Soon a group of history lovers formed the Landmarks Club. They started to raise money to **restore**, or fix up, the missions.

In 1899, Mission San Gabriel church was still used for weekly services.

SAN GABRIEL ARCÁNGEL

The church at San Gabriel was in good condition compared to other mission churches. For years, few changes were made. Other parts of the mission were in ruins. In 1908, Father Raymond Catalan and a group of priests worked carefully. They uncovered old walls, floor tiles, and parts of the mission's water system.

Since then, many buildings at the mission have been restored. An earthquake in 1987 closed the church for five years. Another quake in 1994 caused new damage. Workers continue to repair, restore, and strengthen the buildings. Visitors can see the church, cemetery, winery, and other workshops. A museum contains many items from the original mission.

In the late 1800s, photographers began to remind Americans of the beauty of the crumbling missions. This photo shows San Buenaventura.

SAN BUENAVENTURA

The church at San Buenaventura also remained in good condition. But in 1893, Father Ciprian Rubio made a number of changes. He made the building more modern. He made the windows larger. He covered the floor and ceiling with wood. He also tore out the original wooden pulpit. He painted over the original paintings on the walls. Later, a group of priests, led by Father Aubrey J. O'Reilly, restored the walls, floor, and windows.

The modern-day church of San Buenaventura sits on a busy street in the city of Ventura. The stations of the cross paintings still hang there.

Edwin Deakin painted San Buenaventura after Father Ciprian Rubio's changes.

Visitors to nearby museums can see the foundations of some of the other mission buildings. They can also see pottery and other items.

Many missions were almost completely ruined by weather and treasure hunters. Little remained of Mission San Fernando.

SAN FERNANDO REY DE ESPAÑA

By the 1890s, little was left of Mission San Fernando. In 1916, the Landmarks Club raised money to save it. An expert in adobe construction made thousands of adobe bricks. Other workers replaced the church's tile floor. They rebuilt the bell tower and uncovered old paintings.

But in 1971, an earthquake destroyed the church. An exact copy of the church was built in 1974. Other buildings, including the convento, were damaged by an earthquake in 1994. Still, visitors to this Los Angeles mission can tour the restored buildings and gardens.

Earthquake damage is a serious threat to the remaining missions.

UNDERSTANDING THE MISSIONS

More than two hundred years have passed since Father Junípero Serra started the first mission, San Diego de Alcalá, in California, in 1769. It is a peaceful place in the busy port city of San Diego. Traces of Spanish culture are still easy to see in the area. Red tile roofs and Spanish place-names remind us of this important part of the state's history. The Spaniards brought horses, grapes, and many other good things to the region. But they also brought death and suffering to thousands of Native Americans. We must remember to consider all sides of this amazing story when we visit or read about the California missions.

Many people visit the missions of California each year.

LAYOUTS

These diagrams of the Los Angeles area missions show what the missions look like in modern times. Modern-day missions may not look exactly like the original missions Spanish priests founded. But by studying them, we can get a sense of how neophytes and missionaries lived.

San Gabriel Arcángel: Mission San Gabriel has withstood strong earthquakes since its founding in 1771. During its peak years, the mission produced items to sell.

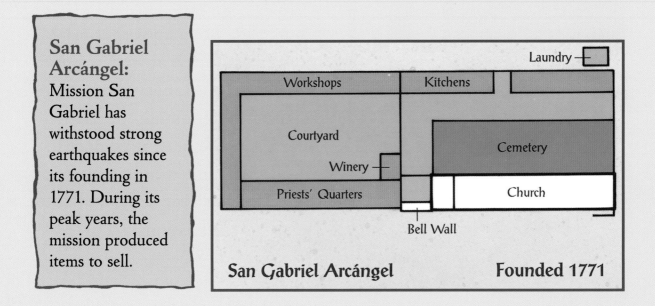

Laundry

Workshops

Kitchens

Courtyard

Cemetery

Winery

Priests' Quarters

Church

Bell Wall

San Gabriel Arcángel   Founded 1771

San Buenaventura: The site for San Buenaventura, a southern mission set up in 1782, was chosen because it was close to coastal Chumash villages.

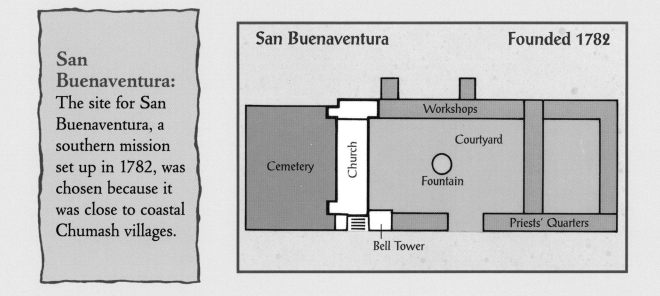

San Buenaventura — Founded 1782

Cemetery · Church · Workshops · Courtyard · Fountain · Bell Tower · Priests' Quarters

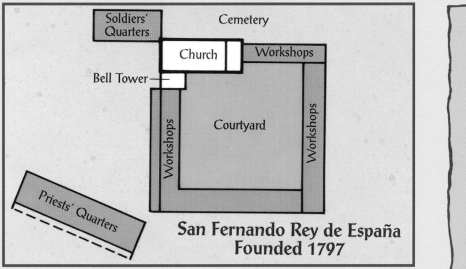

San Fernando Rey de España
Founded 1797

Soldiers' Quarters · Cemetery · Church · Workshops · Bell Tower · Workshops · Courtyard · Workshops · Priests' Quarters

San Fernando Rey de España: Established in 1797, San Fernando Rey de España had facilities for overnight guests and was a favorite stopping place for weary travelers.

TIMELINE

1769   Father Junípero Serra blesses the site of the first California mission, San Diego de Alcalá.

1771   Father Serra founds Mission San Gabriel Arcángel.

1782   Mission San Buenaventura is established.

1784   Father Serra dies. Father Fermín Francisco de Lasuén takes over as father-president of the mission system.

1797   Father Lasuén establishes four new missions.

1810   New Spain goes to war with Spain.

1821   New Spain wins its independence and becomes the Republic of Mexico.

1830s   The Mexican government secularizes the missions.

1846   The United States declares war on Mexico.

1848   Mexico loses the war. The United States takes control of California.

1850   California becomes the thirty-first state.

1860s   The U.S. government returns the missions to the Catholic Church. Mission buildings are falling apart.

1890s   Missions restoration begins. It continues to present times.

GLOSSARY

adobe: bricks made by mixing clay soil with sand, water, and straw

aqueduct: a system of ditches or pipes that carry water

Baja California (lower California): a strip of land off the northwestern coast of Mexico that lies between the Pacific Coast and the Gulf of California

borders: an invisible line that divides one country or region from another

Californios: a settler from Spain or New Spain who made a home in California

convento: a building where priests and other religious people live and work

missionaries: teachers sent out by religious groups to spread their religion to others

missions: centers where religious teachers work to spread their beliefs to other people

neophytes: Native Americans who have joined the Roman Catholic faith and community

New Spain: modern-day Mexico

presidios: Spanish forts for housing soldiers

pueblos: towns

quadrangle: an area or patio surrounded by buildings on four sides

reservations: areas of land the U.S. government set aside for use by Native Americans

restore: to bring something back to its original appearance

secularization: to transfer from religious to nonreligious and state control

PRONUNCIATION GUIDE*

Chumash	CHOO-mash
El Camino Reál	el kah-MEE-no ray-AHL
Lasuén, Fermín Francisco de	lah-soo-AYN, fair-MEEN frahn-SEES-kokh day
San Buenaventura	SAHN BWAY-nah-ven-too-rah
San Fernando Rey de España	SAHN fair-NAHN-doh RAY day es-PAH-nyah
San Gabriel Arcángel	SAHN gah-bree-EHL ar-KAHN-hel
Señán, José	say-NYAN, hoh-SAY
Serra, Junípero	SHE-rrah, hoo-NEE-pay-roh
Tongva	TAHNG-vah
Zalvidea, José María	sahl-vee-DAY-ah, hoh-SAY mah-REE-ah

* Local pronunciations may differ.

TO LEARN MORE

Behrens, June. *Central Coast Missions in California*. Minneapolis: Lerner Publications Company, 2008. Learn all about the missions of California's central coast.

Mission San Buenaventura
http://www.athanasius.com/camission/ventura.htm
This web page provides photos of San Buenaventura as well as a brief history.

Mission San Fernando Rey de España
http://www.athanasius.com/camission/fernando.htm
View photos of the mission and read a brief history.

Mission San Gabriel Arcángel
http://www.athanasius.com/camission/gabriel.htm
View photos of the mission and read a brief history.

Mission San Gabriel Arcángel
http://www.eusd4kids.org/mission_trail/SGabrielArcangel/SGabrielArcangel.html
This website, created by a fourth-grade class, offers a virtual field trip.

Nelson, Libby. *California Mission Projects and Layouts*. Minneapolis: Lerner Publications Company, 2008. This book provides guides for building mission models. It also offers layouts of California's twenty-one missions.

Sonneborn, Liz. *The Chumash*. Minneapolis: Lerner Publications Company, 2007. This book introduces the Chumash in California.

Tongva Indian Memorial and Exhibit
http://www.Imu.edu/Page5460.aspx
This website gives a brief history of the Tongva along with a timeline.

INDEX